KETOGENIC
BREAD MACHINE

TABLE OF CONTENTS

INTRODUCTION

Thank you for purchasing our ketogenic bread machine cookbook.

We have been making bread for over 20 years, but since going keto, we struggled to find recipes that worked in a bread maker.

We bought at least five cookbooks claiming to be ketogenic bread machine recipes. However, none worked. The recipes were cakey, didn't rise, fell apart, or ultimately failed. We wasted a lot of money on not only the books but the ingredients too.

We set ourselves a mission to create recipes that we loved and made weekly. After countless hours and months of development, we started creating and adapting recipes that work in the bread machine!

All of the photos in this book are taken by us.

We hope you love the recipes as much as we do.

Happy baking!

CHAPTER 1

BENEFITS AND RISKS OF A KETOGENIC DIET

Low-carb diets like keto have been the subject of debate for decades. Some people insist that this kind of diet increases cholesterol levels, thereby causing heart conditions because of the high-fat content. A lot of scientific studies, however, prove that low-carb diets have their health benefits.

Benefits:

- Curbs appetite

Dieting often leads to extreme hunger. It is one of the main reasons why people who try to diet eventually give in. However, a keto diet is different because it often leads to a reduction of appetite. Some studies prove that when people cut on their carb intake and eat more fat and protein, they are consuming fewer calories.

- May lead to eventual weight loss

Reducing your carbohydrate intake is one of the easiest and most effective ways to lose weight. Some studies show people who are on low-carb diets like keto tend to lose weight faster than those who are on a low-fat regimen, even when low-fat diets restrict calorie intake.

Low-carb diets get rid of excess water from the body, resulting in decreased insulin levels, leading to faster weight loss just one or two weeks into the keto diet regimen.

- The bigger chunk of fat loss comes from the abdominal cavity

One factor that determines how fat affects your overall health and risk of getting sick is where fat is stored. There are two main types of fat:

Subcutaneous fat – which is located under the skin

Visceral fat – which is found in the abdominal cavity

The majority of obese or overweight people have visceral fat.

Visceral fat is likely to accumulate around your organs. An excess amount of visceral fat is linked to insulin resistance and inflammation, which could potentially cause metabolic dysfunction, also referred to as metabolic syndrome.

Metabolic dysfunction is a cluster of conditions that may occur simultaneously, increasing the risk of developing heart conditions, a stroke, and type 2 diabetes. Conditions include increased blood sugar level, high blood pressure, abnormal levels of cholesterol and triglycerides, and excess body fat accumulation around the waist.

Low-carb diets are effective in reducing harmful abdominal fat. Studies show that most of the fat that people lose while on a low-carb diet seems to have been accumulated in the abdominal cavity.

- Triglycerides levels dramatically decrease

Triglycerides are fat molecules circulating in the bloodstream.

One of the main causes of elevated triglycerides levels in sedentary people is carb consumption, particularly fructose, which is a simple sugar.

- Helps increase "good" HDL cholesterol levels

HDL or high-density lipoprotein is more commonly known as "good" cholesterol. The higher the levels of HDL to the levels of "bad" LDL, the lower the risk of you getting heart disease. The keto diet allows you to eat a lot of fat, which is one way to increase the levels of HDL.

- May help regulate "bad" LDL cholesterol levels

If you have high levels of LDL, you are most likely to suffer a heart attack. But according to doctors, the size of the particles is integral. Smaller particles are said to put you at a higher risk of heart ailments, while large particles may lower LDL levels.

Studies show that a keto diet may increase the size of cholesterol particles while decreasing the number of total LDL particles in the bloodstream. Hence, lowering your intake of carbohydrates may help boost your heart health.

- May help reduce blood sugar and insulin levels

The keto diet may be able to help people suffering from diabetes and insulin resistance. Studies show that reducing carb intake drastically lowers blood sugar and insulin levels.

If you're taking medications, especially to regulate blood sugar levels, make sure that you consult with your doctor before going into any kind of diet plan. Your doctor might make a few changes in your dosage requirement to avoid hypoglycemia.

- May help lower blood pressure

Hypertension or elevated blood pressure may cause many different medical conditions, including kidney failure, heart ailments, and stroke. A reduced intake of carbohydrates may help in regulating blood pressure levels, thus reducing the risk of developing these conditions, thus helping you live longer.

- May help prevent metabolic syndrome

Metabolic syndrome has symptoms that may include elevated blood pressure, abdominal obesity, high levels of triglycerides, increased fasting blood sugar levels, and low HDL levels.

A keto diet may effectively address all of these symptoms.

- May be therapeutic for some brain disorders

The brain needs glucose because there are parts of the brain that can only burn this type of sugar.

A large percentage of the brain can burn the ketones that are formed during starvation or fasting, or when carb intake is reduced. This is the actual principle behind the keto diet. The ketogenic diet has been used as a treatment for epilepsy in children who don't respond to drug treatment.

Studies continue how keto and low-carb diets may work in the prevention and treatment of other brain disorders like Parkinson's and Alzheimer's diseases.

Risks:

Briefly, here are some of the known dangers of following the keto diet:

- Keto "flu."

Symptoms may include gastrointestinal stress, vomiting, fatigue, and lethargy. But this keto "flu" passes after a few days. Doctors say that about 25% of those who try to do a keto diet experience symptoms of keto "flu."

The most common symptom is extreme fatigue.

Dieters are often asked to increase liquid (especially water) intake to minimize these negative side effects of this diet. Getting enough sleep is also key.

- Diarrhea

Many people experience diarrhea while on the ketogenic diet. This may be because the gallbladder becomes "overwhelmed" in producing bile that will be broken down into fat.

Diarrhea may also be an indication that there is not enough fiber in your keto diet. Intolerance to dairy or artificial sweeteners might also be the reason.

- Ketoacidosis

It is not advisable to follow the keto diet if you are diagnosed with type 1 or type 2 diabetes without consulting your doctor, and doing so under close supervision and monitoring. Ketosis can be helpful for those who have hyperglycemia. However, you will have to check your blood glucose levels several times a day.

Researchers say that for people who have diabetes, the process of ketosis potentially triggers ketoacidosis, which is a dangerous condition. This happens when the body stores up too many ketones (these are acids that are byproducts of the fat burning process). The body is likely to become more acidic, resulting in damages in the brain, liver, and kidneys. If left untreated, this condition could be fatal.

CHAPTER 2

INTRODUCTION TO
THE BREAD MACHINE

Most bread machines have different programs to make a variety of different loaves and cakes. This is excellent for making keto bread.

Get To Know Your Bread Machine

Take time to familiarize yourself with the machine. There should be a hinged lid that can be lifted and shut, a window to see into the pan, and a small vent. Next to the lid, there should be a control panel with the function buttons.

Inside the bread machine, you'll see a bread pan or bread bucket with a handle. It works as a mixing bowl and baking pan. There is a little bread paddle or kneading blade found at the center of the bucket. It should be removed once the baking is done. Both the bread bucket and blade are removable.

Familiarize Yourself with the Settings

The control panel contains the display screen and the function buttons. You might find these buttons:

Select
Stop/Start
Crust Color
Timer or Arrow

When you plug in the machine, it will automatically be on the default setting, which is the Basic button.

When you choose the Select button, you'll find several choice settings on what kind of bread you intend to make. The most common choices would be:

White or Basic
Whole Wheat
French
Pizza
Multigrain

You will find a Bake mode option (Bake, Bake Rapid, Dough, Sandwich). This button will determine the sequence of mixing, kneading, rising, and then baking. For instance, you chose the Dough mode. The machine will stop without cooking the dough. At this point, you will have to open the lid and remove the dough. After which you will take it out for reshaping and cooking in the oven.

You will simply press on the Select button until you reach the desired setting.

There is also the size setting button – Small, Medium, Large, X-Large (sometimes it will also be in terms of loaf size, e.g., 1.5lb, 2lb)

You will also find the Crust setting (which is not available in every machine). If there is a Crust button in your machine, there will be three settings to choose from – Light, Medium, Dark. The machine will always start on the default setting, which is Medium. Normally, the Crust button won't work until you have selected the dough cycle and before you press the Start button.

When using the Timer button, refer to the recipe you want to follow. Once you've secured the bread bucket in the machine and you have closed the lid, you should select the cycle that is needed. You can use the Arrow buttons when adjusting the time on the display screen.

You'll press the Start button to start baking your bread.

You don't need to monitor the cooking time because you already set the timer and the cycle setting.

Bread Machine Paddle

Most bread machines come with two paddle options, the 'Classic Paddle' and what is commonly known as the 'Rye Kneading Paddle'.

We recommend using the 'Classic Paddle' for all ketogenic bread loaves. This is because the dough tends to be thicker than that of traditional bread. We have tried using both, and the 'Rye Kneading Paddle' tends to get stuck in the bread and doesn't mix it so well.

CLASSIC PADDLE

RYE KNEADING PADDLE

CHAPTER 3

BASIC KETOGENIC FOOD LIST

Followers of the ketogenic diet attest that this low-carb, high-fat diet plan helps in weight loss. Here is a list of the food that is ideal for keto and those that you should avoid.

What You Should Eat While On A Keto Diet:

Meat
Pork, chicken (dark meat), beef, venison, lamb, turkey (dark meat), ham, bacon, sausage (in moderation)

Fats and Oils
Butter, olive oil, coconut oil, ghee, avocado oil, lard, mayonnaise

Vegetables
Cabbage, broccoli, cauliflower, pepper, zucchini, eggplant, tomato, cucumber, asparagus, mushroom, onion, spinach, green beans, olives, lettuce

High-Fat Dairy
Cheese, cream cheese, sour cream, heavy cream

Nuts
Peanuts, almonds, pecans, macadamia nuts, walnuts, hazelnuts, almond butter, peanut butter

Seafood
Snapper, salmon, tuna, trout, cod, halibut, catfish, oysters, clams, crab, scallops, mussels, lobsters

Berries (but sparingly)
Raspberries, blackberries, blueberries

Artificial sweeteners (but sparingly)
Sucralose, stevia, erythritol

Alcohol (but sparingly)
Hard liquor

Eggs
Any kind

Spices
Any kind

Coffee
Unsweetened

What You Should Avoid While On A Keto Diet:

Fruits
Bananas, oranges, grapes, apples, peaches, watermelon, cherries, pineapple, melon, pears, plums, mangoes, grapefruits

Grains and Starches
Rice, wheat, rye, corn, quinoa, oats, barley, bulgur, amaranth, millet, sprouted greens, buckwheat

Root Vegetables
Yams, carrots, beets, turnips, potatoes (regular and sweet), parsnips, yuca

Grain Products
Bread, pasta, oatmeal, pizza, crackers, cereal, granola, popcorn, muesli, flour, bagels

Legumes
Kidney beans, black beans, pinto beans, soybeans, lentils, chickpeas, peas

Sweeteners
Cane sugar, maple syrup, agave, aspartame, nectar

Sweets
Chocolates, candies, cakes, pastries, pies, tarts, ice cream, cookies, buns, custard, pudding

Some oil
Soybean oil, canola oil, sesame oil, peanut oil, grapeseed oil, sunflower oil

Alcohol
Beer, sweet wine, cider, sweetened alcoholic drinks

Sweetened Beverages
Smoothies, artificial juice, soda, sweetened tea, sweetened coffee

Low-fat dairy
Skim milk, fat-free yogurt, skim mozzarella,

Sweetened Sauces and Dips
Barbecue sauce, ketchup, tomato sauce, hot sauce, some salad dressings

CHAPTER 4

KETOGENIC BREAD MACHINE INGREDIENTS

Keto bread requires some ingredients to be altered from regular bread recipes. Here are some ingredients that you can use to make keto bread with your bread machine.

Almond Flour

Almond flour is finely ground blanched almonds. It's an excellent source of vitamin E. Almonds are rich in iron, calcium, magnesium, manganese, and potassium. It gives a nutty flavor, moist, and slightly dense character to your bread. If you're familiar with French macarons, they are usually made with almond flour. It is ideal for baking bread, cookies, and cakes.

It is one of the best grain-free substitutes for regular flour. Almond flour is a low-carb staple for people on the keto diet. A 1/4 cup contains 5 grams of protein, 12 grams of fat, and only 2 grams of net carbs. Almond flour has high-fat content but low on gluten, so you might need to add more eggs or baking powder to make sure that your bread will have more structure.

This is readily available in grocery stores and supermarkets. It is available online, and you can make huge savings when you buy in bulk.

Coconut Flour

Coconut flour comes from the dehydrated coconut meat after most of its fat content has been extracted to produce coconut oil.

Since coconut flour is high in fiber, it is recommended for anyone who wants to boost their digestive health.

Similar to almond flour, coconut flour cannot be substituted directly in your old recipe collection. Coconut flour is different altogether from all the other nut flours as it can soak up the liquid and absorb moisture like a sponge.

You can use coconut flour for baking keto bread in many different ways:

- Substitute 1/4 to 1/3 cup coconut flour for 1 cup of regular all-purpose flour.
- You can bake coconut flour using the same temperature as other bread recipes, and there is no need to make adjustments.
- For 1 1/2 cups of coconut flour, use 1 1/2 cup of liquid and 7 eggs.

Oat Fiber

Oat fiber may come as a surprise since this is not your usual keto recipe ingredient. It is an insoluble fiber that is made from grinding oat hulls, the shell that coats the oat groat (kernel). Whole oat groats are from harvesting oats, then washing them, and finally removing the hulls. The groat is a popular source of most oat products that you normally use in your kitchen. However, not like rolled oats, steel-cut oats, etc., oat fiber is made 100% from the husks.

It is important to mention that oat fiber doesn't have many nutritional benefits, and it is non-digestible. Though, it is not normally consumed for its vitamins and minerals.

It is ideal for making keto bread because it does not contain net carbs. What is a net carb? It is the product that is left after taking fiber away from the total amount of carbs from your food.

Vital Wheat Gluten

Like oat fiber, vital wheat gluten is not a popular keto ingredient.

First off, the food you eat while on a keto diet does not necessarily mean it has to be gluten-free. Vital wheat gluten has a high protein content but low in carbohydrates. 1 tablespoon of vital wheat gluten only has 1 gram of carbohydrate, which is ideal for incorporating into a low-carb diet like ketogenic.

Health experts also say that vital wheat gluten is less likely to cause a huge increase in blood sugar levels.

When used for baking, it can give keto flour the body and structure needed to make doughs that are "close to the real thing". It is an important ingredient that your recipe might need to add a little bit of texture and structure to the bread or any other baked goodies.

Flaxseed

Ground flaxseed is also known as flax meal, ground flax, or linseed. Flaxseeds are extremely nutritious and are excellent sources of copper, vitamin B1, lignans (or plant compounds that help prevent cell damage caused by free radicals), and ALA (or plant-derived omega 3s).

For every 2 tablespoons of ground flax, it has about 70 calories, 5 grams total carbs, 4.5 grams fat, 4 grams fiber, 1 gram net carbs, and 3 grams protein.

Its earthy taste makes it a good choice to make keto-friendly bread, cookies, muffins, scones, and nutty cakes. It may not be typically used in keto recipes, but flaxseed has many other uses, and one important use is that it can replace eggs in your recipes. You'll only need to mix flaxseeds with water and let the mixture "swell", and then the flaxseeds will exhibit egg-like properties. However, you cannot use this technique when the recipe needs a significant amount of eggs.

Xanthan Gum

Xanthan gum works as a binder to hold all the bread ingredients together. It is an important ingredient in many low carb baked products. You'll only need just 1/2 teaspoon for a lot of different recipes.

Aside from acting as a binder, it is also a good alternative for gluten when making bread. Gluten makes bread rise as it traps air bubbles. Xanthan gum can also do just that.

Xanthan gum mimics the function of gluten, but it doesn't serve as leavener (yeast). It makes the dough sticky and gummy, allowing the dough to trap the fast bubbles from yeast (or other leavener, such as baking soda). This will also allow the dough to rise. Imagine a big piece of bubble gum.

It is a good alternative for gelatin powder, guar gum, ground flaxseed, and psyllium husk. These ingredients all work as a binder.

Erythritol

Erythritol is a sweet keto ingredient. It is a sugar alcohol or polyol, which is about 60 to 80% as sweet as table sugar (sucrose). Erythritol is naturally found in minor amounts in fruits like grape, pear, and watermelon. There is erythritol in mushrooms, fermented drinks like beer and wine, and even in soy sauce.

It has long been used as a brown or white sugar substitute. It is a byproduct of fermented corn or cornstarch.

Erythritol can be partially absorbed and digested by the intestinal tract, occasionally triggering gastrointestinal discomfort.

It does not contain sugars or calories, making it a good keto bread ingredient. It is a good alternative to regular sugar as it is granulated. It will not raise your insulin or blood sugar levels.

It does not have the same "mouth feel" as regular sugar, it gives a cooling sensation on the tongue.

Unfortunately, it will not react with the yeast to make the bread rise, as sugar would do. But it is great to add to loaves to make them sweeter.

Psyllium Husk

Psyllium husk is a kind of seed that is commercially produced for use as dietary fiber. The small husk is known as a good fiber-rich binding agent. When you mix psyllium husk with liquid, the consistency changes to thick and gluey. They expand up to 10 times their original size.

It has long been used to help cleanse the colon. When used in cooking, it makes an excellent binder. Using psyllium husk produces a good crumb-like texture for the bread. This is why psyllium husk is an important ingredient when you want to make low-carb bread, pastries, cakes, cookies, and pies.

This ingredient makes keto bread almost the same as regular wheat bread because it has a whole wheat texture and flavor but without the unwanted net carbs.

Baking Powder

Baking powder is a dry chemical agent. It is produced when an acid (monocalcium phosphate, or cream of tartar, or aluminum sulfate) is mixed with sodium bicarbonate (which is more popularly known as baking soda).

Liquid substances like water may cause a chemical reaction that will produce carbon dioxide, which will then get trapped in minute air pockets in the batter or dough. The application of heat will release additional carbon monoxide, thereby expanding the trapped carbon dioxide gas and air, consequently creating steam. The process will be exerted as the trapped air pockets expand, causing the batter or dough to rise.

It is mainly used as a leavening agent, which allows the dough to rise. You can easily find it in grocery stores and supermarkets. It also makes a good substitute for yeast.

Take note that baking powder does not in any way enhance the flavor of the food. It just triggers a chemical reaction that makes bread, cakes, and cookies rise.

Yeast

Yeast is a single-cell fungus that can only be seen under the microscope. It has the shape of an egg. One gram of yeast is about 20 billion yeast cells. They grow when yeast cells begin breaking down food. The process also allows them to replenish their energy.

Yeast acts as a leavener. It ferments the sugar and then releases carbon dioxide. The resulting dough will be stretchable and elastic; thus, carbon dioxide won't be able to escape. The expanding gas will cause the dough to rise.

Yeast is also used in making beer. It consumes the sugar in beer to produce alcohol and carbon dioxide.

There are 2 kinds of yeast:

- Brewer's yeast - This is a wet yeast that is primarily used in making beer.
- Baker's yeast - This is used as a leavening agent in baking. There are 2 types of baker's yeast; dry yeast, and fresh yeast. Fresh yeast (or wet) comes in small, square-shaped cases that are made from fresh yeast cells. These are often used by professional bakers. It is 70% moisture and easily perishable.

There are 2 types of dry yeast. These are active dry yeast and instant yeast. Their only difference is the size of the granules – active yeast granules are larger, and instant yeast has a fine texture.

In this book, we use 'easy-bake' yeast, also commonly known as 'easy-blend' or 'fast-action' yeast.

Honey

Honey may have a lot of health benefits, but it is not normally used as a keto ingredient. Raw honey has many nutritional benefits. It is a good antioxidant and serves as a healthier alternative to sugar.

Raw honey is a pure, thick, golden liquid. It is unfiltered and a natural sweetener that is produced by bees from the nectar of flowers. The nectar is the sweet juice from the flower that the bee takes and stores in the stomach. There are two stomachs in a bee's body, one is used for eating, and the other is used for carrying nectar back to their hive.

Sugar and honey are digested differently. There is a special enzyme to raw honey, and this is broken down into two sugar molecules so it can immediately utilize it for energy. As for table sugar, the body will have to break down the sugar molecules with the use of enzymes before it can be used for energy.

A tablespoon of raw honey has 17 grams net carbs, 16 are from sugar. It has 0 grams fat, has no dietary fiber, and contains just 1/10 gram protein. Being high carb, it makes sense that this is not ideal for the keto diet.

However, in some recipes, it is essential to make the bread rise. Yeast will need sugar to react. Normally, only 1 tsp is used for an entire loaf.

And remember that ketosis is a metabolic state. You can consume about 20 to 25 grams of total carbs a day and remain in the ketosis state. Athletes and active people can consume up to 100 grams of carbs a day and be in ketosis.

Flavorings

On a keto diet, you can use flavorings for your food. Here are some of the acceptable flavorings and spices for a keto diet:

- Dried herbs that have low-carb content are thyme, coriander, mint, cinnamon, ginger, basil, and tarragon. Paprika, cayenne, oregano, and cumin contain slightly more carbs, but they are still good for keto but only in smaller amounts.
- Garam masala is a traditional Indian spice. It gives food the spicy kick. It has cumin, cloves, black pepper, coriander, nutmeg, and cinnamon.
- Turmeric, curry powder, pumpkin spice, onion powder, and garlic granules are also good for keto.

- Vinegar only has 1 gram carbs per 1 tablespoon.
- Soy sauce and balsamic vinegar have under 3 grams of carbs per 1 tablespoon.

Ketogenic Bread Recipes

Before we get into the recipes, a few notes:

Bread Machine: The bread machine we have and have used for every recipe is the Panasonic SD-ZB2502. If you have an alternative model, the size/setting will need to be altered accordingly. We have tried to keep the options as diverse as possible. But this is the machine we have tested the recipes in.

Measurements: We have both grams and cups for measurements. Grams are far more accurate, and we believe they create a better loaf. Electric scales are affordable, and we think a well worth investment. However, if you only own cups, we have added the approximate measurements.

Nutritional Information: All of the nutritional information included in the book is based on the exact brand of ingredients we used. However, different brands do have different nutritional information, so please be aware they may vary slightly. If you have any concerns, please contact us, and we can send you the nutritional breakdown for each loaf.

Difficulty: Keto bread is more complex to make than regular bread. We have found that keto bread often requires the ingredients to be mixed before being placed in the bread maker. Or additional steps outside of the bread machine. This is how we have created the most consistent loaves. However, if you do not have the time, you can try combining the ingredients in the bread pan, but we have found inconsistent results thus far.

Ingredients: We have tried to use similar ingredients throughout the book for consistency, affordability, and ease. When making loaves from other books, we found that each recipe had a huge variety of ingredients. This made it more expensive and meant we needed a lot of storage space. Hopefully, we have made the recipes simple, affordable, and as easy as possible. It also means you can bulk buy the ingredients and make a nice saving.

Sweetness: It is important to note that honey is used in some of these recipes. The yeast requires sugar to make the bread rise. The amount of honey used in the recipes is so minute that it does not drastically alter the nutritional information. Therefore, the bread is still in line with the ketogenic diet. Unfortunately, low-carb sweeteners do not have the same effect.

CHAPTER 5

CLASSIC KETOGENIC
BREAD RECIPES

We have adapted and developed 3 basic recipes, oat bread, coconut bread, and almond bread.

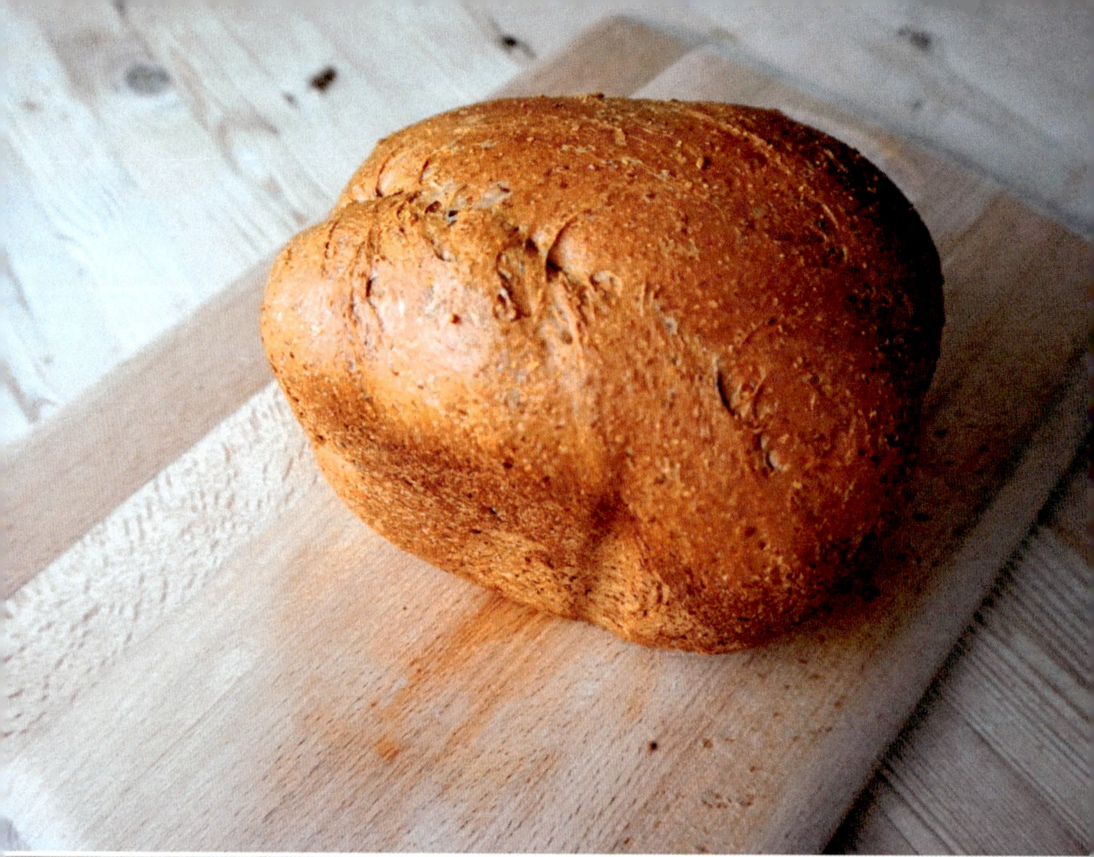

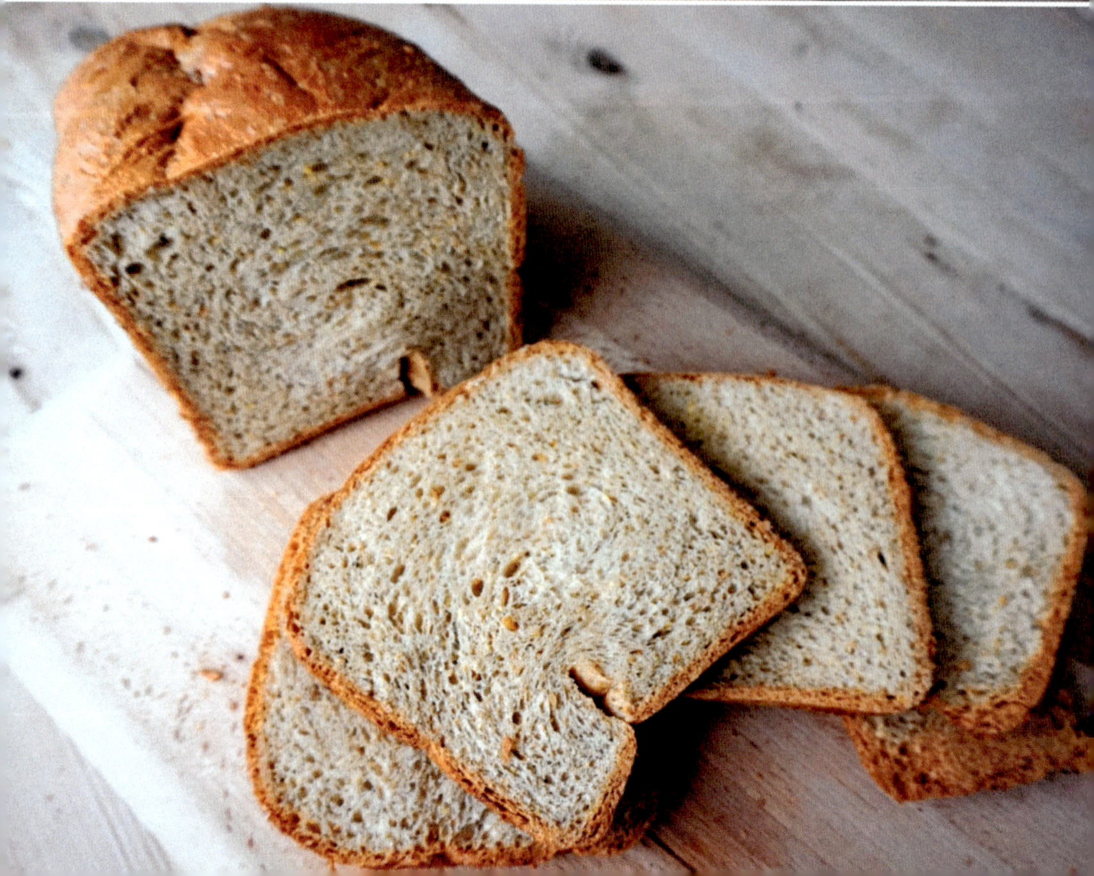

OAT LOAF

This is the most versatile and most similar to regular wheat bread. It's great with lots of different savory flavor combinations.

Slices: 12

Nutrition Information (per loaf):

Calories:	*1226*
Total Fat:	*42g*
Total Carbohydrates:	*89.7g*
Of Which Sugars:	*8.4g*
Dietary Fiber:	*70.3g*
Protein:	*166.2g*

Nutrition Information (per slice):

Calories:	*102*
Total Fat:	*3.5g*
Total Carbohydrates:	*7.4g*
Of Which Sugars:	*0.7g*
Dietary Fiber:	*5.8g*
Protein:	*13.8g*

Ingredients:

- 45g (1/2 cup) oat fiber
- 70g (2/3 cup) flaxseed meal
- 170g (1 1/4 cup) vital wheat gluten
- 1/2 tsp xanthan gum
- 1/2 tsp salt
- 250ml (1 cup) warm water
- 1 tsp honey
- 2 eggs
- 1 tbsp easy bake yeast

Directions:

1. In a bowl, combine oat fiber, flaxseed meal, vital wheat gluten, xanthan gum, and salt. Thoroughly mix. Add the mix into the bread maker.
2. In a separate bowl, add the warm water and the honey. Stir until the honey is dissolved. Add the eggs and whisk until the eggs are blended in. Add to the bread machine.
3. Sprinkle the yeast over the top of the mixes.
4. Set your bread maker to the BASIC setting, select the largest size, sometimes this is 2lb or XL, depending on your machine, and DARK for the crust color. The cycle should be 3-4 hours in a standard bread maker.
5. Once complete, remove from the bread maker and allow it to cool before slicing.

ALMOND LOAF

Almond bread is a great alternative for sandwiches. It's a softer loaf than regular bread and works great to adapt to sweeter loaves.

Slices: 14

Nutrition Information (per loaf):		*Nutrition Information (per slice):*	
Calories:	*2171*	*Calories:*	*155*
Total Fat:	*191.8g*	*Total Fat:*	*13.7g*
Total Carbohydrates:	*65.8g*	*Total Carbohydrates:*	*4.7g*
Of Which Sugars:	*9g*	*Of Which Sugars:*	*0.6g*
Dietary Fiber:	*32.5g*	*Dietary Fiber:*	*2.3g*
Protein:	*81.3g*	*Protein:*	*5.8g*

Ingredients:

- 230g (2 cups) almond flour
- 35g (1/3 cup) flaxseed meal
- 1 tsp salt
- 1 tbsp baking powder
- 45g (1/4 cup) melted coconut oil
- 4 eggs
- 187ml (3/4 cup) water

Directions:

1. In a bowl, combine almond flour, flaxseed meal, salt, and baking powder. Thoroughly mix. Add to the bread maker.
2. Combine the melted oil, eggs, and water. Mix until the eggs are whisked. Add to the bread machine.
3. Set your bread maker to the RAPID/QUICK setting, select the largest size, sometimes this is 2lb or XL, depending on your machine, and DARK for the crust color. The cycle should be 1.5-2 hours in a standard bread maker.
4. Once complete, remove from the bread maker and allow it to cool before slicing.

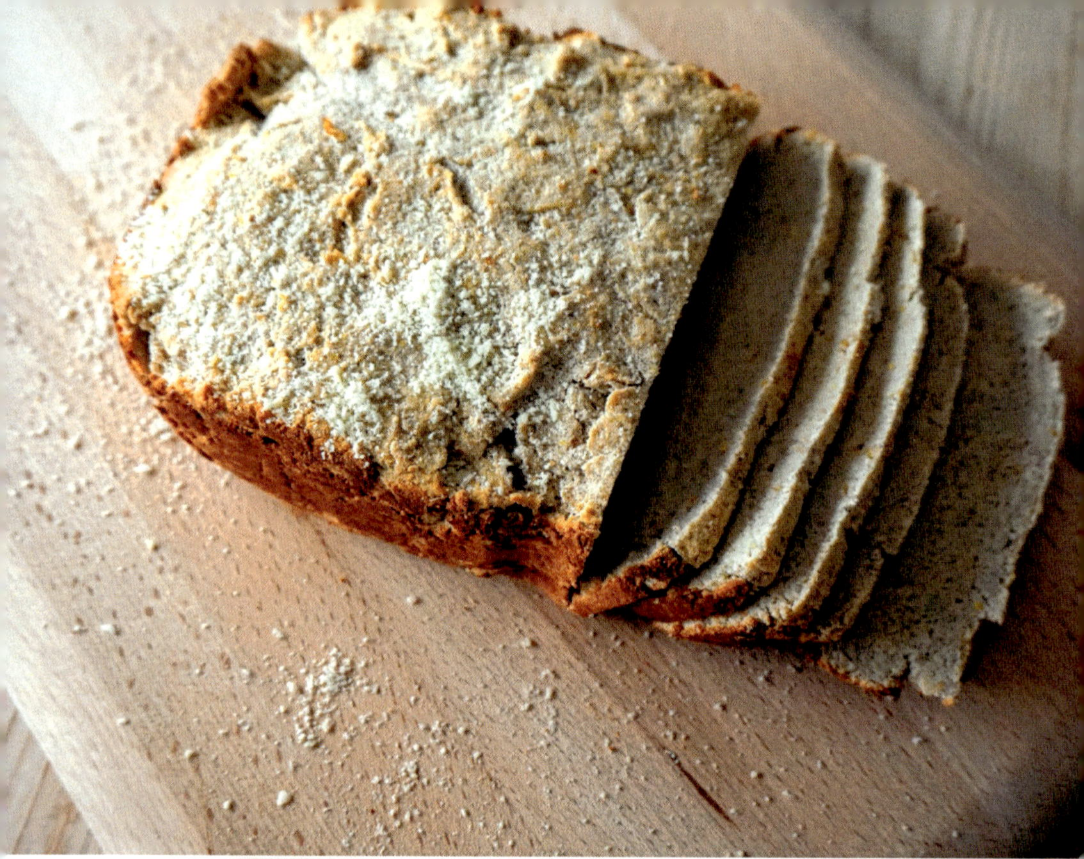

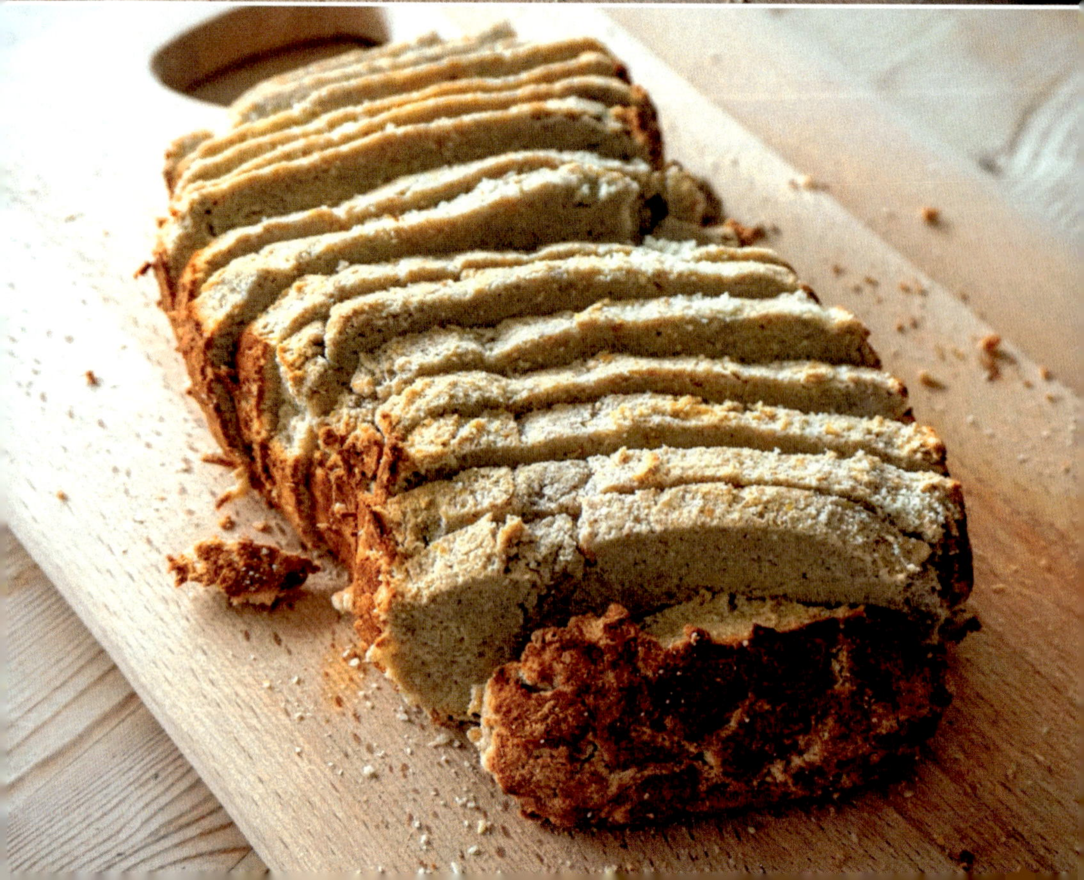

COCONUT LOAF

Coconut bread is denser and sweeter than other bread. It is delicious toasted with butter.

Slices: 15

Nutrition Information (per loaf):

Calories:	*1940*
Total Fat:	*113g*
Total Carbohydrates:	*156.3g*
Of Which Sugars:	*34.3g*
Dietary Fiber:	*115.4g*
Protein:	*75.9g*

Nutrition Information (per slice):

Calories:	*129*
Total Fat:	*7.5g*
Total Carbohydrates:	*10.4g*
Of Which Sugars:	*2.2g*
Dietary Fiber:	*7.6g*
Protein:	*5g*

Ingredients:

- 180g (1 1/2 cup) coconut flour
- 30g (1/4 cup) flaxseed meal
- 40g (1/4 cup) ground psyllium husk
- 1 tsp salt
- 45g (1/4 cup) melted coconut oil
- 7 eggs
- 1 tsp honey
- 375ml (1 1/2 cups) warm water
- 1 tsp easy bake yeast

Directions:

1. In a bowl, combine the coconut flour, flaxseed meal, psyllium husk, and salt. Mix thoroughly.
2. To a separate bowl, add the melted oil, eggs, honey, and water. Mix until the eggs are whisked.
3. Combine the dry and wet mixes.
4. Sprinkle the mixture with yeast.
5. Stir the dough until well combined. Then use your hands to knead the dough until it comes together into a ball, you can pick it up, and it stays stuck together.
6. Place the dough ball in the bread pan and flatten with the palm of your hand.
7. Bake the dough on the BAKE ONLY setting for 55 minutes.
8. Once complete, remove from the bread maker and allow it to cool before slicing.

Flavored Recipes

The next few chapters consist of flavored loaves. These loaves are adaptations of our original recipes.

We have tried various flours and meals, but have found sticking to known recipes to be the most successful.

CHAPTER 6

SAVORY VEGETARIAN KETOGENIC BREAD RECIPES

HERBY OLIVE LOAF

Slices: 12

Nutrition Information (per loaf):

Calories:	1429
Total Fat:	61.4g
Total Carbohydrates:	91.5g
Of Which Sugars:	10.1g
Dietary Fiber:	75.6g
Protein:	168.4g

Nutrition Information (per slice):

Calories:	119
Total Fat:	5.1g
Total Carbohydrates:	7.6g
Of Which Sugars:	0.8g
Dietary Fiber:	6.3g
Protein:	14g

Ingredients:

- 45g (1/2 cup) oat fiber
- 70g (2/3 cup) flaxseed meal
- 170g (1 1/4 cup) vital wheat gluten
- 1/2 tsp xanthan gum
- 1/2 tsp salt
- 1 tsp garlic granules
- 1/2 tbsp dried basil
- 1/2 tbsp dried thyme
- 250ml (1 cup) warm water
- 1 tsp honey
- 2 eggs
- 120g (1 1/2 cups) pitted black olives
- 1 tbsp easy bake yeast

Directions:

1. In a bowl, combine oat fiber, flaxseed meal, vital wheat gluten, xanthan gum, salt, garlic granules, basil, and thyme. Thoroughly mix. Add the mix into the bread maker.
2. In a separate bowl, add the warm water and the honey. Stir until the honey is dissolved. Add the eggs and whisk until the eggs are blended in. Add to the bread machine.

3. Add the olives.
4. Sprinkle the yeast over the top of the mixes.
5. Set your bread maker to the BASIC setting, select the largest size, sometimes this is 2lb or XL, depending on your machine, and DARK for the crust color. The cycle should be 3-4 hours in a standard bread maker.
6. Once complete, remove from the bread maker and allow it to cool before slicing.

CURRY AND COCONUT LOAF

Slices: 15

Nutrition Information (per loaf):

Calories:	*1973*
Total Fat:	*114.1g*
Total Carbohydrates:	*159.1g*
Of Which Sugars:	*34.9g*
Dietary Fiber:	*118.2g*
Protein:	*77.1g*

Nutrition Information (per slice):

Calories:	*131*
Total Fat:	*7.6g*
Total Carbohydrates:	*10.6g*
Of Which Sugars:	*2.3g*
Dietary Fiber:	*7.8g*
Protein:	*5.1g*

Ingredients:

- 180g (1 1/2 cup) coconut flour
- 30g (1/4 cup) flaxseed meal
- 40g (1/4 cup) ground psyllium husk
- 1 tsp salt
- 1 tbsp curry powder
- 1/2 tsp cumin
- 1/2 tsp turmeric powder
- 45g (1/4 cup) melted coconut oil
- 7 eggs
- 1 tsp honey
- 375ml (1 1/2 cups) warm water
- 1 tsp easy bake yeast

Directions:

1. In a bowl, combine the coconut flour, flaxseed meal, psyllium husk, salt, curry powder, cumin, and turmeric. Mix thoroughly.
2. To a separate bowl, add the melted oil, eggs, honey, and water. Mix until the eggs are whisked.
3. Combine the dry and wet mixes.
4. Add the yeast.
5. Stir the dough until well combined. Then use your hands to knead the dough until it comes together into a ball, you can pick it up, and it stays stuck together.
6. Place the dough ball in the bread pan and flatten with the palm of your hand.
7. Bake the dough on the BAKE ONLY setting for 55 minutes.
8. Once complete, remove from the bread maker and allow it to cool before slicing.

GARLIC AND ROSEMARY LOAF

Slices: 12

Nutrition Information (per loaf):		*Nutrition Information (per slice):*	
Calories:	*1251*	*Calories:*	*104*
Total Fat:	*46.6g*	*Total Fat:*	*3.8g*
Total Carbohydrates:	*92.3g*	*Total Carbohydrates:*	*7.6g*
Of Which Sugars:	*8.6g*	*Of Which Sugars:*	*0.7g*
Dietary Fiber:	*70.9g*	*Dietary Fiber:*	*5.9g*
Protein:	*167.4g*	*Protein:*	*13.9g*

Ingredients:

- 14g or 2 garlic cloves
- 5g (1 tsp) coconut oil
- 45g (1/2 cup) oat fiber
- 70g (2/3 cup) flaxseed meal
- 170g (1 1/4 cup) vital wheat gluten
- 1/2 tsp xanthan gum
- 1/2 tsp salt
- 1 tsp ground black pepper
- 1/2 tbsp chopped fresh rosemary
- 250ml (1 cup) warm water
- 1 tsp honey
- 2 eggs
- 1 tbsp easy bake yeast

Directions:

1. Chop the garlic and fry in the 1 tsp coconut oil until fragrant. Set aside.
2. In a bowl, combine oat fiber, flaxseed meal, vital wheat gluten, xanthan gum, salt, black pepper, and rosemary. Thoroughly mix. Add the mix into the bread maker.
3. In a separate bowl, add the warm water and the honey. Stir until the honey is dissolved. Add the eggs and whisk until the eggs are blended in. Add to the bread machine.
4. Add the fried garlic.
5. Sprinkle the yeast over the top of the mixes.
6. Set your bread maker to the BASIC setting, select the largest size, sometimes this is 2lb or XL, depending on your machine, and DARK for the crust color. The cycle should be 3-4 hours in a standard bread maker.
7. Once complete, remove from the bread maker and allow it to cool before slicing.

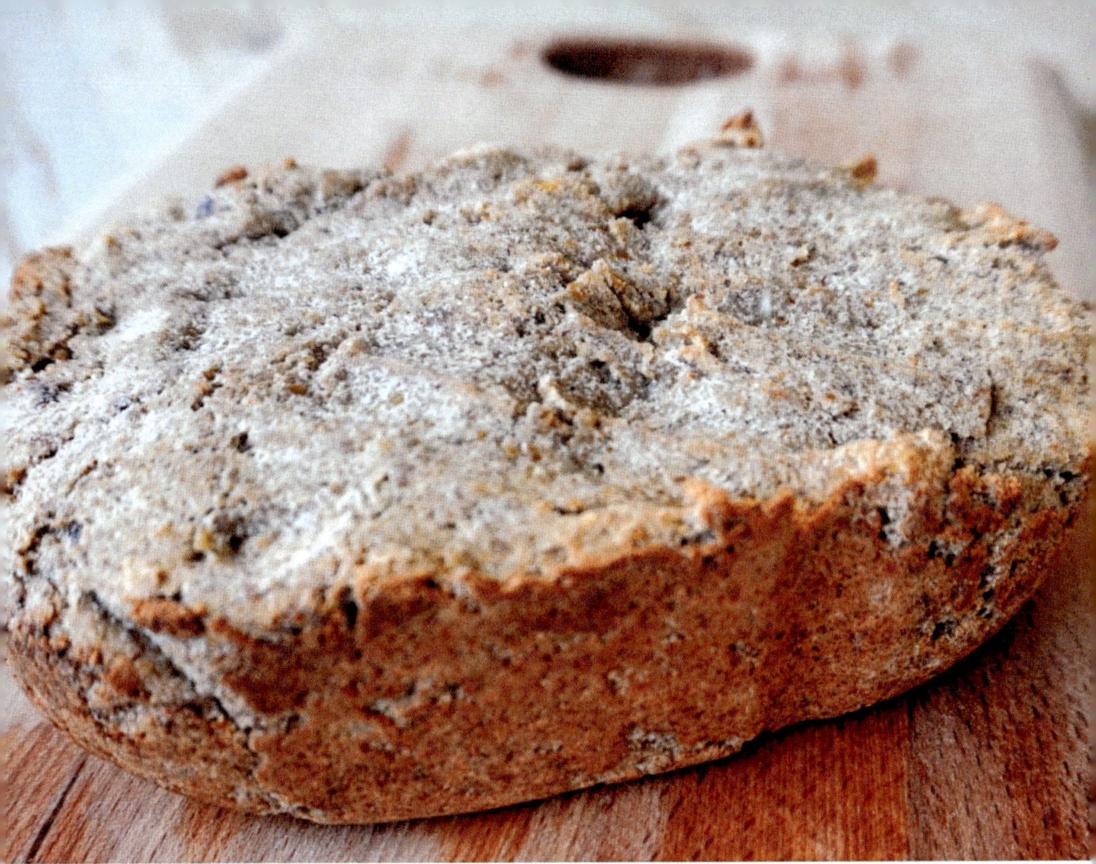

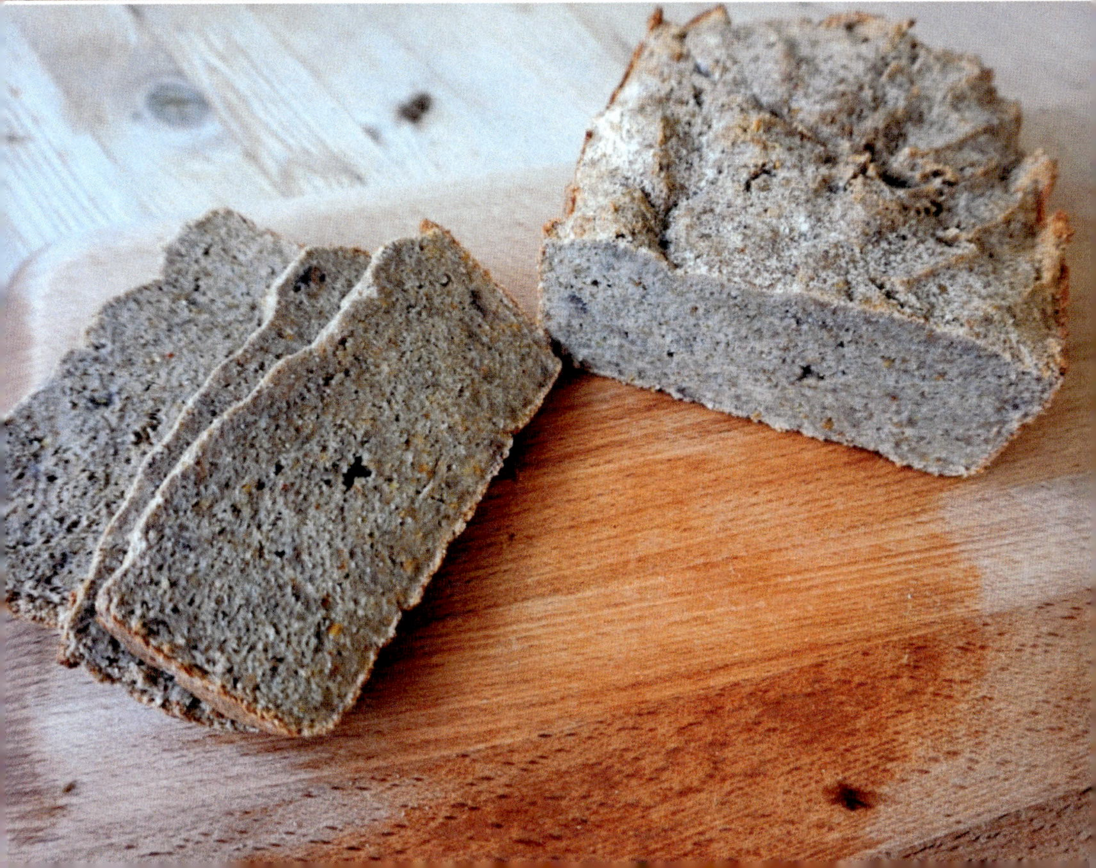

CHILI AND COCONUT LOAF

Slices: 15

Nutrition Information (per loaf):

Calories:	1955
Total Fat:	113.4g
Total Carbohydrates:	158.2g
Of Which Sugars:	34.7g
Dietary Fiber:	115.4g
Protein:	76.5g

Nutrition Information (per slice):

Calories:	130
Total Fat:	7.5g
Total Carbohydrates:	10.5g
Of Which Sugars:	2.3g
Dietary Fiber:	7.6g
Protein:	5.1g

Ingredients:

- 180g (1 1/2 cup) coconut flour
- 30g (1/4 cup) flaxseed meal
- 40g (1/4 cup) ground psyllium husk
- 1 tsp salt
- 1-2 tsp chili powder
- 1/2 tsp paprika
- 1 tsp garlic granules
- 1/2 tsp cumin
- 45g (1/4 cup) melted coconut oil
- 7 eggs
- 1 tsp honey
- 375ml (1 1/2 cups) warm water
- 1 tsp easy bake yeast

Directions:

1. In a bowl, combine the coconut flour, flaxseed meal, psyllium husk, salt, chili powder, paprika, garlic granules, and cumin. Mix thoroughly.
2. To a separate bowl, add the melted oil, eggs, honey, and water. Mix until the eggs are whisked.
3. Combine the dry and wet mixes.
4. Add the yeast.
5. Stir the dough until well combined. Then use your hands to knead the dough until it comes together into a ball, you can pick it up, and it stays stuck together.
6. Place the dough ball in the bread pan and flatten with the palm of your hand.
7. Bake the dough on the BAKE ONLY setting for 55 minutes.
8. Once complete, remove from the bread maker and allow it to cool before slicing.

CHEESE AND JALAPEÑO LOAF

Slices: 12

Nutrition Information (per loaf):		*Nutrition Information (per slice):*	
Calories:	*1492*	*Calories:*	*124*
Total Fat:	*61g*	*Total Fat:*	*5g*
Total Carbohydrates:	*96.1g*	*Total Carbohydrates:*	*8g*
Of Which Sugars:	*10.8g*	*Of Which Sugars:*	*0.9g*
Dietary Fiber:	*72.4g*	*Dietary Fiber:*	*6g*
Protein:	*182.3g*	*Protein:*	*15.1g*

Ingredients:

- 45g (1/2 cup) oat fiber
- 70g (2/3 cup) flaxseed meal
- 170g (1 1/4 cup) vital wheat gluten
- 1/2 tsp xanthan gum
- 1/2 tsp salt
- 1 tsp garlic granules
- 250ml (1 cup) warm water
- 1 tsp honey
- 2 eggs
- 150g (3/4 cup) sliced jalapeños
- 50g (1/2 cup) cheddar cheese, grated/shredded
- 1 tbsp easy bake yeast

Directions:

1. In a bowl, combine oat fiber, flaxseed meal, vital wheat gluten, xanthan gum, salt, and garlic granules. Thoroughly mix. Add the mix into the bread maker.
2. In a separate bowl, add the warm water and the honey. Stir until the honey is dissolved. Add the eggs and whisk until the eggs are blended in. Add to the bread machine.
3. Add the jalapeños and cheddar cheese.
4. Sprinkle the yeast over the top of the mixes.
5. Set your bread maker to the BASIC setting, select the largest size, sometimes this is 2lb or XL, depending on your machine, and DARK for the crust color. The cycle should be 3-4 hours in a standard bread maker.
6. Once complete, remove from the bread maker and allow it to cool before slicing.

SEEDED LOAF

Slices: 14

Nutrition Information (per loaf):

Calories:	2385
Total Fat:	210.6g
Total Carbohydrates:	69.7g
Of Which Sugars:	10.8g
Dietary Fiber:	35.8g
Protein:	88g

Nutrition Information (per slice):

Calories:	170
Total Fat:	15g
Total Carbohydrates:	4.9g
Of Which Sugars:	0.7g
Dietary Fiber:	2.5g
Protein:	6.2g

Ingredients:

- 230g (2 cups) almond flour
- 35g (1/3 cup) flaxseed meal
- 1 tsp salt
- 1 tbsp baking powder
- 45g (1/4 cup) melted coconut oil
- 4 eggs
- 187ml (3/4 cup) water
- 20g (1/8 cup) sesame seeds
- 15g (1/8 cup) sunflower seeds

Directions:

1. In a bowl, combine almond flour, flaxseed meal, salt, and baking powder. Thoroughly mix. Add to the bread maker.
2. Combine the melted oil, eggs, and water. Mix until the eggs are whisked. Add to the bread machine.
3. Add the sesame and sunflower seeds.
4. Set your bread maker to the RAPID/QUICK setting, select the largest size, sometimes this is 2lb or XL, depending on your machine, and DARK for the crust color. The cycle should be 1.5-2 hours in a standard bread maker.
5. Once complete, remove from the bread maker and allow it to cool before slicing.

CHEESE, TOMATO, AND HERB LOAF

Slices: 12

Nutrition Information (per loaf):
Calories: 2341
Total Fat: 127.1g
Total Carbohydrates: 117.5g
   Of Which Sugars: 22.6g
Dietary Fiber: 70.3g
Protein: 219.4g

Nutrition Information (per slice):
Calories: 195
Total Fat: 10.5g
Total Carbohydrates: 9.7g
   Of Which Sugars: 1.8g
Dietary Fiber: 5.8g
Protein: 18.2g

Ingredients:

- 45g (1/2 cup) oat fiber
- 70g (2/3 cup) flaxseed meal
- 170g (1 1/4 cup) vital wheat gluten
- 1/2 tsp xanthan gum
- 1/2 tsp salt
- 1 tsp dried mixed herbs, e.g., oregano, parsley, thyme, basil
- 250ml (1 cup) warm water
- 1 tsp honey
- 2 eggs
- 150g (1 cup) sun-dried tomatoes
- 100g (1 cup) cheddar cheese, grated/shredded
- 50g (1/4 cup) hard cheese, shredded/grated
- 1 tbsp easy bake yeast

Directions:

1. In a bowl, combine oat fiber, flaxseed meal, vital wheat gluten, xanthan gum, salt, and mixed herbs. Thoroughly mix. Add the mix into the bread maker.
2. In a separate bowl, add the warm water and the honey. Stir until the honey is dissolved. Add the eggs and whisk until the eggs are blended in. Add to the bread machine.
3. Chop the sun-dried tomatoes into 1/2-inch square pieces. Place the tomatoes and cheeses into the bread maker.
4. Sprinkle the yeast over the top of the mixes.
5. Set your bread maker to the BASIC setting, select the largest size, sometimes this is 2lb or XL, depending on your machine, and DARK for the crust color. The cycle should be 3-4 hours in a standard bread maker.
6. Once complete, remove from the bread maker and allow it to cool before slicing.

CHEESE AND ONION LOAF

Slices: 12

Nutrition Information (per loaf):

Calories:	1726
Total Fat:	83.5g
Total Carbohydrates:	100.6g
Of Which Sugars:	13.4g
Dietary Fiber:	71.6g
Protein:	195.5g

Nutrition Information (per slice):

Calories:	144
Total Fat:	6.9g
Total Carbohydrates:	8.3g
Of Which Sugars:	1.1g
Dietary Fiber:	5.9g
Protein:	16.2g

Ingredients:

- 1 medium red onion
- 5g (1 tsp) coconut oil
- 45g (1/2 cup) oat fiber
- 70g (2/3 cup) flaxseed meal
- 170g (1 1/4 cup) vital wheat gluten
- 1/2 tsp xanthan gum
- 1/2 tsp salt
- 250ml (1 cup) warm water
- 1 tsp honey
- 2 eggs
- 100g (1 cup) cheddar cheese, grated/shredded
- 1 tbsp easy bake yeast

Directions:

1. Dice the onion and fry in the coconut oil until soft and fragrant. Set aside.
2. In a bowl, combine oat fiber, flaxseed meal, vital wheat gluten, xanthan gum, and salt. Thoroughly mix. Add the mix into the bread maker.
3. In a separate bowl, add the warm water and the honey. Stir until the honey is dissolved. Add the eggs and whisk until the eggs are blended in. Add to the bread machine.
4. Add the onion and cheese to the bread maker.
5. Sprinkle the yeast over the top of the mixes.
6. Set your bread maker to the BASIC setting, select the largest size, sometimes this is 2lb or XL, depending on your machine, and DARK for the crust color. The cycle should be 3-4 hours in a standard bread maker.
7. Once complete, remove from the bread maker and allow it to cool before slicing.

HERBED COCONUT LOAF

Slices: 15

Nutrition Information (per loaf):		*Nutrition Information (per slice):*	
Calories:	*1976*	*Calories:*	*131*
Total Fat:	*117.4g*	*Total Fat:*	*7.8g*
Total Carbohydrates:	*160.7g*	*Total Carbohydrates:*	*10.7g*
Of Which Sugars:	*35g*	*Of Which Sugars:*	*2.3g*
Dietary Fiber:	*116.6g*	*Dietary Fiber:*	*7.7g*
Protein:	*78.4g*	*Protein:*	*5.2g*

Ingredients:

- 5g (1 tsp) coconut oil
- 28g or 4 garlic cloves
- 180g (1 1/2 cup) coconut flour
- 30g (1/4 cup) flaxseed meal
- 40g (1/4 cup) ground psyllium husk
- 1 tsp salt
- 1/2 tsp dried basil
- 1/2 tsp dried oregano
- 45g (1/4 cup) melted coconut oil
- 7 eggs
- 1 tsp honey
- 375ml (1 1/2 cups) warm water
- 1 tsp easy bake yeast

Directions:

1. Slice the garlic cloves and fry in the 1 tsp coconut oil until fragrant. Set aside.
2. In a bowl, mix the coconut flour, flaxseed meal, psyllium husk, salt, basil, and oregano. Mix thoroughly.
3. To a separate bowl, add the melted oil, eggs, honey, and water. Mix until the eggs are whisked.
4. Combine the dry and wet mixes.
5. Sprinkle the mixture with yeast.
6. Stir the dough until well combined. Then use your hands to knead the dough until it comes together into a ball, you can pick it up, and it stays stuck together.
7. Place the dough ball in the bread pan and flatten with the palm of your hand.
8. Bake the dough on the BAKE ONLY setting for 55 minutes.
9. Once complete, remove from the bread maker and allow it to cool before slicing.

CHEESY GARLIC LOAF

Slices: 12

Nutrition Information (per loaf):

Calories:	*1725*
Total Fat:	*83.5g*
Total Carbohydrates:	*96.9g*
Of Which Sugars:	*9.7g*
Dietary Fiber:	*71.7g*
Protein:	*197.1g*

Nutrition Information (per slice):

Calories:	*143*
Total Fat:	*6.9g*
Total Carbohydrates:	*8g*
Of Which Sugars:	*0.8g*
Dietary Fiber:	*5.9g*
Protein:	*16.4g*

Ingredients:

- 35g or 5 garlic cloves
- 5g (1 tsp) coconut oil
- 45g (1/2 cup) oat fiber
- 70g (2/3 cup) flaxseed meal
- 170g (1 1/4 cup) vital wheat gluten
- 1/2 tsp xanthan gum
- 1/2 tsp salt
- 1 tsp garlic granules
- 250ml (1 cup) warm water
- 1 tsp honey
- 2 eggs
- 100g (1 cup) cheddar cheese, grated/shredded
- 1 tbsp easy bake yeast

Directions:

1. Slice the garlic cloves and fry in the 1 tsp coconut oil until fragrant. Set aside.
2. In a bowl, combine oat fiber, flaxseed meal, vital wheat gluten, xanthan gum, salt, and garlic granules. Thoroughly mix. Add the mix into the bread maker.
3. In a separate bowl, add the warm water and the honey. Stir until the honey is dissolved. Add the eggs and whisk until the eggs are blended in. Add to the bread machine.
4. Add the fried garlic and cheese to the bread maker.
5. Sprinkle the yeast over the top of the mixes.
6. Set your bread maker to the BASIC setting, select the largest size, sometimes this is 2lb or XL, depending on your machine, and DARK for the crust color. The cycle should be 3-4 hours in a standard bread maker.
7. Once complete, remove from the bread maker and allow it to cool before slicing.

CHAPTER 7

MEATY KETOGENIC BREAD RECIPES

HAM AND MUSTARD LOAF

Slices: 12

Nutrition Information (per loaf):		Nutrition Information (per slice):	
Calories:	*1591*	*Calories:*	*132*
Total Fat:	*64.8g*	*Total Fat:*	*5.4g*
Total Carbohydrates:	*93.2g*	*Total Carbohydrates:*	*7.7g*
Of Which Sugars:	*9.8g*	*Of Which Sugars:*	*0.8g*
Dietary Fiber:	*71.4g*	*Dietary Fiber:*	*5.9g*
Protein:	*202.5g*	*Protein:*	*16.8g*

Ingredients:

- 45g (1/2 cup) oat fiber
- 70g (2/3 cup) flaxseed meal
- 170g (1 1/4 cup) vital wheat gluten
- 1/2 tsp xanthan gum
- 1/2 tsp salt
- 1 tsp ground black pepper
- 2g (1/2 tbsp) mustard powder
- 250ml (1 cup) warm water
- 1 tsp honey
- 2 eggs
- 50g (1/2 cup) cheddar cheese, grated/shredded
- 115g (3/4 cup) ham slices, cut into 1/2-inch squares
- 1 tbsp easy bake yeast

Directions:

1. In a bowl, combine oat fiber, flaxseed meal, vital wheat gluten, xanthan gum, salt, black pepper, and mustard powder. Thoroughly mix. Add the mix into the bread maker.
2. In a separate bowl, add the warm water and the honey. Stir until the honey is dissolved. Add the eggs and whisk until the eggs are blended in. Add to the bread machine.
3. Add the ham and cheese to the bread maker.
4. Sprinkle the yeast over the top of the mixes.
5. Set your bread maker to the BASIC setting, select the largest size, sometimes this is 2lb or XL, depending on your machine, and DARK for the crust color. The cycle should be 3-4 hours in a standard bread maker.
6. Once complete, remove from the bread maker and allow it to cool before slicing.

CHEESE AND BACON LOAF

Slices: 12

Nutrition Information (per loaf):

Calories:	2343
Total Fat:	131.2g
Total Carbohydrates:	92.2g
Of Which Sugars:	10.1g
Dietary Fiber:	71.4g
Protein:	215g

Nutrition Information (per slice):

Calories:	195
Total Fat:	10.9g
Total Carbohydrates:	7.6g
Of Which Sugars:	0.8g
Dietary Fiber:	5.9g
Protein:	17.9g

Ingredients:

- 230g (1 cup) bacon lardons, or cubed bacon
- 45g (1/2 cup) oat fiber
- 70g (2/3 cup) flaxseed meal
- 170g (1 1/4 cup) vital wheat gluten
- 1/2 tsp xanthan gum
- 1/2 tsp salt
- 250ml (1 cup) warm water
- 1 tsp honey
- 2 eggs
- 100g (1 cup) cheddar cheese, shredded/grated
- 1 tbsp easy bake yeast

Directions:

1. Dry fry the chunks of bacon until cooked through. Set aside.
2. In a bowl, combine oat fiber, flaxseed meal, vital wheat gluten, xanthan gum, and salt. Thoroughly mix. Add the mix into the bread maker.
3. In a separate bowl, add the warm water and the honey. Stir until the honey is dissolved. Add the eggs and whisk until the eggs are blended in. Add to the bread machine.
4. Add the cooked bacon and shredded cheese.
5. Sprinkle the yeast over the top of the mixes.
6. Set your bread maker to the BASIC setting, select the largest size, sometimes this is 2lb or XL, depending on your machine, and DARK for the crust color. The cycle should be 3-4 hours in a standard bread maker.
7. Once complete, remove from the bread maker and allow it to cool before slicing.

CHEESE AND CHORIZO LOAF

Slices: 12

Nutrition Information (per loaf):		*Nutrition Information (per slice):*	
Calories:	*1659*	*Calories:*	*138*
Total Fat:	*76.7g*	*Total Fat:*	*6.3g*
Total Carbohydrates:	*92.4g*	*Total Carbohydrates:*	*7.7g*
Of Which Sugars:	*9.9g*	*Of Which Sugars:*	*0.8g*
Dietary Fiber:	*70.9g*	*Dietary Fiber:*	*5.9g*
Protein:	*192.9g*	*Protein:*	*16g*

Ingredients:

- 60g (1/2 cup) diced chorizo
- 45g (1/2 cup) oat fiber
- 70g (2/3 cup) flaxseed meal
- 170g (1 1/4 cup) vital wheat gluten
- 1/2 tsp xanthan gum
- 1/2 tsp salt
- 1/2 tsp smoked paprika
- 250ml (1 cup) warm water
- 1 tsp honey
- 2 eggs
- 50g (1/2 cup) cheddar cheese, grated/shredded
- 1 tbsp easy bake yeast

Directions:

1. Dry fry the chorizo until cooked through. Set aside.
2. In a bowl, combine oat fiber, flaxseed meal, vital wheat gluten, xanthan gum, salt, and paprika. Thoroughly mix. Add the mix into the bread maker.
3. In a separate bowl, add the warm water and the honey. Stir until the honey is dissolved. Add the eggs and whisk until the eggs are blended in. Add to the bread machine.
4. Add the cooked chorizo and shredded cheese.
5. Sprinkle the yeast over the top of the mixes.
6. Set your bread maker to the BASIC setting, select the largest size, sometimes this is 2lb or XL, depending on your machine, and DARK for the crust color. The cycle should be 3-4 hours in a standard bread maker.
7. Once complete, remove from the bread maker and allow it to cool before slicing.

CHAPTER 8

SWEET KETOGENIC BREAD RECIPES

COFFEE AND PECAN LOAF

Slices: 14

Nutrition Information (per loaf):		*Nutrition Information (per slice):*	
Calories:	*2585*	*Calories:*	*184*
Total Fat:	*235g*	*Total Fat:*	*16.7g*
Total Carbohydrates:	*84.3g*	*Total Carbohydrates:*	*6g*
Of Which Sugars:	*11.4g*	*Of Which Sugars:*	*0.8g*
Polyols:	*10g*	*Polyols:*	*0.7g*
Dietary Fiber:	*38.5g*	*Dietary Fiber:*	*2.7g*
Protein:	*86.7g*	*Protein:*	*6.1g*

Ingredients:

- 187ml (3/4 cup) water
- 20g (4 tbsp) strong instant coffee granules
- 60g (1/2 cup) pecans
- 230g (2 cups) almond flour
- 35g (1/3 cup) flaxseed meal
- 1 tsp salt
- 1 tbsp baking powder
- 10g (1 tbsp) erythritol
- 45g (1/4 cup) melted coconut oil
- 4 eggs

Directions:

1. Boil the water in a pan. Once boiling, add the coffee and stir. Set aside to cool.
2. Grind the pecans in a food processor or chop finely.
3. In a bowl, combine almond flour, flaxseed meal, salt, baking powder, erythritol, and chopped pecans. Thoroughly mix. Add into the bread maker.
4. In a separate bowl, combine the coffee, melted oil, and eggs. Mix until the eggs are whisked. Add to the bread machine.
5. Set your bread maker to the RAPID/QUICK setting, select the largest size, sometimes this is 2lb or XL, depending on your machine, and DARK for the crust color. The cycle should be 1.5-2 hours in a standard bread maker.
6. Once complete, remove from the bread maker and allow it to cool before slicing.

LEMON AND POPPY SEED LOAF

Slices: 14

Nutrition Information (per loaf):		*Nutrition Information (per slice):*	
Calories:	*2301*	*Calories:*	*164*
Total Fat:	*200.2g*	*Total Fat:*	*14.3g*
Total Carbohydrates:	*116.8g*	*Total Carbohydrates:*	*8.3g*
Of Which Sugars:	*16g*	*Of Which Sugars:*	*1.1g*
Polyols:	*40g*	*Polyols:*	*2.85g*
Dietary Fiber:	*35.9g*	*Dietary Fiber:*	*2.5g*
Protein:	*86.5g*	*Protein:*	*6.1g*

Ingredients:

- 230g (2 cups) almond flour
- 35g (1/3 cup) flaxseed meal
- 1 tsp salt
- 1 tbsp baking powder
- 40g (4 tbsp) erythritol
- 18g (2 tbsp) poppy seeds
- 1-2 lemons, zest and juice
- 45g (1/4 cup) melted coconut oil
- 4 eggs
- 187ml (3/4 cup) water

Directions:

1. In a bowl, combine almond flour, flaxseed meal, salt, baking powder, erythritol, poppy seeds, and lemon zest. Thoroughly mix. Add into the bread maker.
2. Combine the melted oil, eggs, lemon juice, and water. Mix until the eggs are whisked. Add to the bread machine.
3. Set your bread maker to the RAPID/QUICK setting, select the largest size, sometimes this is 2lb or XL, depending on your machine, and DARK for the crust color. The cycle should be 1.5-2 hours in a standard bread maker.
4. Once complete, remove from the bread maker and allow it to cool before slicing.

COCONUT AND CINNAMON LOAF

Slices: 15

Nutrition Information (per loaf):

Calories:	2039
Total Fat:	122.3g
Total Carbohydrates:	197.7g
Of Which Sugars:	35.3g
Polyols:	40g
Dietary Fiber:	117.1g
Protein:	76.8g

Nutrition Information (per slice):

Calories:	136
Total Fat:	8.1g
Total Carbohydrates:	13.1g
Of Which Sugars:	2.3g
Polyols:	2.6g
Dietary Fiber:	7.8g
Protein:	5.1g

Ingredients:

- 180g (1 1/2 cup) coconut flour
- 30g (1/4 cup) flaxseed meal
- 40g (1/4 cup) ground psyllium husk
- 1 tsp salt
- 15g (1/8 cup) desiccated coconut
- 1 tsp ground cinnamon
- 40g (4 tbsp) erythritol
- 45g (1/4 cup) melted coconut oil
- 7 eggs
- 1 tsp honey
- 375ml (1 1/2 cups) warm water
- 1 tsp easy bake yeast

Directions:

1. In a bowl, mix the coconut flour, flaxseed powder, psyllium husk, salt, desiccated coconut, cinnamon, and erythritol. Mix thoroughly.
2. To a separate bowl, add the melted oil, eggs, honey, and water. Mix until the eggs are whisked.
3. Combine the dry and wet mixes.
4. Sprinkle the mixture with yeast.
5. Stir the dough until well combined. Then use your hands to knead the dough until it comes together into a ball, you can pick it up, and it stays stuck together.
6. Place the dough ball in the bread pan and flatten with the palm of your hand.
7. Bake the dough on the BAKE ONLY setting for 55 minutes.
8. Once complete, remove from the bread maker and allow it to cool before slicing.

ALMOND SPICE LOAF

Slices: 14

Nutrition Information (per loaf):	
Calories:	*2182*
Total Fat:	*192g*
Total Carbohydrates:	*106.9g*
Of Which Sugars:	*9.2g*
Polyols:	*40g*
Dietary Fiber:	*32.5g*
Protein:	*81.5g*

Nutrition Information (per slice):	
Calories:	*155*
Total Fat:	*13.7g*
Total Carbohydrates:	*7.6g*
Of Which Sugars:	*0.6g*
Polyols:	*2.85g*
Dietary Fiber:	*2.3g*
Protein:	*5.8g*

Ingredients:

- 230g (2 cups) almond flour
- 35g (1/3 cup) flaxseed meal
- 1 tsp salt
- 1 tbsp baking powder
- 1 tsp ground cinnamon
- 1/2 tsp ground nutmeg
- 1/4 tsp ground ginger
- 40g (4 tbsp) erythritol
- 45g (1/4 cup) melted coconut oil
- 4 eggs
- 187ml (3/4 cup) water

Directions:

1. In a bowl, combine almond flour, flaxseed meal, salt, baking powder, cinnamon, nutmeg, ginger, and erythritol. Thoroughly mix. Add to the bread maker.
2. Combine the melted oil, eggs, and water. Mix until the eggs are whisked. Add to the bread machine.
3. Set your bread maker to the RAPID/QUICK setting, select the largest size, sometimes this is 2lb or XL, depending on your machine, and DARK for the crust color. The cycle should be 1.5-2 hours in a standard bread maker.
4. Once complete, remove from the bread maker and allow it to cool before slicing.

LEMON AND BLUEBERRY LOAF

Slices: 14

Nutrition Information (per loaf):

Calories:	2231
Total Fat:	193g
Total Carbohydrates:	106.2g
Of Which Sugars:	19.8g
Polyols:	30g
Dietary Fiber:	32.5g
Protein:	83.7g

Nutrition Information (per slice):

Calories:	159
Total Fat:	13.7g
Total Carbohydrates:	7.5g
Of Which Sugars:	1.4g
Polyols:	2.1g
Dietary Fiber:	2.3g
Protein:	5.9g

Ingredients:

- 230g (2 cups) almond flour
- 35g (1/3 cup) flaxseed meal
- 1 tsp salt
- 1-2 lemons, zest and juice
- 30g (3 tbsp) erythritol
- 1 tbsp baking powder
- 45g (1/4 cup) melted coconut oil
- 4 eggs
- 187ml (3/4 cup) water
- 50g (1/2 cup) blueberries

Directions:

1. In a bowl, combine almond flour, flaxseed meal, salt, lemon zest, erythritol, and baking powder. Thoroughly mix. Add to the bread maker.
2. Combine the melted oil, eggs, lemon juice, and water. Mix until the eggs are whisked. Add to the bread machine.
3. Add the blueberries.
4. Set your bread maker to the RAPID/QUICK setting, select the largest size, sometimes this is 2lb or XL, depending on your machine, and DARK for the crust color. The cycle should be 1.5-2 hours in a standard bread maker.
5. Once complete, remove from the bread maker and allow it to cool before slicing.

PUMPKIN SEED SPICE LOAF

Slices: 14

Nutrition Information (per loaf):

Calories:	2367
Total Fat:	205.8g
Total Carbohydrates:	71.3g
Of Which Sugars:	10.6g
Dietary Fiber:	34.9g
Protein:	91.4g

Nutrition Information (per slice):

Calories:	169
Total Fat:	14.7g
Total Carbohydrates:	5g
Of Which Sugars:	0.7g
Dietary Fiber:	2.4g
Protein:	6.5g

Ingredients:

- 230g (2 cups) almond flour
- 35g (1/3 cup) flaxseed meal
- 1 tsp salt
- 1 tbsp baking powder
- 1/2 tsp ground cinnamon
- 1/4 tsp ground ginger
- 1/4 tsp ground cloves
- 45g (1/4 cup) melted coconut oil
- 4 eggs
- 187ml (3/4 cup) water
- 30g (1/4 cup) pumpkin seeds

Directions:

1. In a bowl, combine almond flour, flaxseed meal, salt, baking powder, cinnamon, ginger, and cloves. Thoroughly mix. Add to the bread maker.
2. Combine the melted oil, eggs, and water. Mix until the eggs are whisked. Add to the bread machine.
3. Add the pumpkin seeds.
4. Set your bread maker to the RAPID/QUICK setting, select the largest size, sometimes this is 2lb or XL, depending on your machine, and DARK for the crust color. The cycle should be 1.5-2 hours in a standard bread maker.
5. Once complete, remove from the bread maker and allow it to cool before slicing.

CONCLUSION

I hope you loved the recipes as much as we did.

Feel free to experiment with different flavors to find the perfect loaf for you. Make sure to share your findings with us and others following a ketogenic diet.

We understand that it is not your everyday recipe book, with 100's of recipes. However, as previously mentioned, we wanted to produce successful ketogenic bread in the bread machine.

I hope this book is worthy of your positive feedback.

Now you can have your bread, and eat it too.

Manufactured by Amazon.ca
Bolton, ON